The temptation to try crack and other drugs may confront students in all kinds of schools.

THE DRUG ABUSE PREVENTION LIBRARY

CRACK

Rodney G. Peck

THE ROSEN PUBLISHING GROUP, INC.
NEW YORK

Published in 1991 by the Rosen Publishing Group, Inc.
29 East 21st Street, New York, NY 10010

Copyright ©1991 by The Rosen Publishing Group, Inc.

First Edition

Manufactured in the United States of America

Library of Congress Cataloging-in-Publication Data

Peck, Rodney G.
    Crack/Rodney G. Peck.—1st ed.
    (The Drug Abuse Prevention Library)
    Includes bibliographical references and index.
    Summary: Discusses the characteristics of crack cocaine
    and the dangers of using the drug.
        ISBN 0-8239-1262-0
        1. Crack (Drug)—Juvenile literature. 2. Cocaine
        habit—Juvenile literature. [1. Crack (Drug)
        2. Cocaine habit. 3. Drug abuse.] I. Title.
        II. Series.
        HV5809.5.P43   1991
        362.29'8—dc20   91-11141
                                                         CIP
                                                          AC

Contents

13.16

Teenagers sometimes try drugs just because they are forbidden.

Drug Dependence

Drugs! They seem to be everywhere these days. We see drugs on the news and in the movies. We hear songs about drugs on the radio and MTV. And we learn about drugs from friends, family, and school. But how much do we know about drugs? How does a person "get hooked" on drugs? How are we affected by our family and friends?

Drug use has to start somewhere. Some people start using drugs just to try them. They experiment with the drug to find out how it feels. They don't think that the drug will hurt them. If they like how the drug makes them feel, they try it again. Then they begin using it regularly. That is how

8 people "get hooked" on crack and other drugs. They think experimenting won't hurt, but it does.

Everyone knows that drugs hurt the body. But how do they hurt the body? As soon as someone takes a drug, the body starts to change.

Paul is a guy who smokes one marijuana joint to get high. After a few months of smoking marijuana, Paul's body has changed. His body has become used to one joint. Now Paul has to smoke two joints to get high.

Linda is a small girl. She gets drunk on two cans of beer. But after a few months of drinking, her body changes. It has become used to two cans of beer. Now Linda needs three or four cans of beer to get drunk.

This change in the body is called *tolerance*. Linda's body has built a tolerance to alcohol. Paul's body has built a tolerance to marijuana. When the body builds tolerance, it needs more and more of a drug to reach the same high as before. That is one way that drugs hurt your body.

The next step in "getting hooked" is easy to fall into. You are already using drugs regularly. Your body has built a tolerance to drugs. Then you start using drugs to celebrate, to relax, to feel at ease around other people, and for lots of other reasons. You need the drug to get through the day. You depend on the drug. That need for the drug is called *chemical dependency.* Drugs are chemicals that change the way your body works.

When you are dependent on a drug, your body and mind need the drug to work normally. You don't have much control over your use of the drug. A drug-dependent person suffers *withdrawal.* Withdrawal is the way the body reacts when it doesn't have the drug. Crack users have withdrawals. They can't sleep. They see things that aren't there. They have trouble breathing.

Drug *addiction* is the last step. The drug use has turned into a disease. Drug users live for the drug. They think about the next time they will have the drug. They think about how much of it they will buy. They think about where they will get it. Drug users are "hooked" on the drug. They live to get high. They depend on the drug to get them there.

Addicts have an uncontrollable urge to use drugs. They have no control over their drug use. They can be addicted to more than one drug at a time too. Addicts use the drug even if it has bad effects.

last ✓ para.

10   Drug dependence or addiction can happen to anyone. It happens to rich people. It happens to poor people. It happens to people of all races. But some people are different. Some people may become dependent on drugs more easily than others:

Brian's mother uses cocaine. Brian's sister is addicted to crack. Brian needs to be careful. Studies show that people like Brian who have family members who are drug addicts are in much greater danger of becoming addicts than people who do not. Brian has the disease of drug addiction in his family. This disease is easily passed from one generation to another. Brian is aware of the danger he is in. Brian chooses not to use drugs because of that danger.

Your family can play a big part in whether or not you will use drugs. Having drugs in your home affects the way you look at them. Parents who use drugs send a bad message that "drugs are O.K." Sisters and brothers who use drugs send the same bad message. So your family has a major influence on your decision to use drugs.

The people you hang out with also play a big part. So do the places that you go.

What if Brian's friends go to parties every
weekend? They go to parties and get high.
Sooner or later he will feel pressure to "fit
in" with his friends. But Brian doesn't
want to be around drugs. He's too smart
for that.

Brian can hang out with other people
who don't do drugs. Together they can do
things that are drug-free. Brian has to
choose which group he wants to be a part
of: the people who use drugs or the people
who don't. It's his choice.

Remember these things: Experimenting
with drugs leads to regular use of drugs.
The body builds tolerance to a drug. Then
it takes more and more of the drug to get
high. Finally, you become chemically dependent or addicted to the drug and have
no control of your use of it. You have no
control of your life.

Everyone who uses a drug is taking a
chance. Someone who has a chemically
dependent or addicted person in the family is taking a big chance of becoming
dependent on drugs. Finally, to be drug-
free, it is important to do things with drug-
free friends and to go to drug-free places.

Even legal drugs become addictive. Some teenagers get hooked on cigarettes.

CHAPTER 2

Legal Drugs: Why Start?

*I*n most states, it is against the law for a person under twenty-one years of age to drink alcohol. It is also against the law for a person under eighteen to buy cigarettes. Many teenagers choose to ignore the laws. That is when drug use starts for many people. It starts when they are teenagers. And it usually starts with drugs such as tobacco and alcohol. Some teenagers also start with marijuana. That drug isn't legal for anyone.

Because alcohol and tobacco are legal, they are easy to get. In one survey, 80 percent of teenagers said that marijuana was also easy to get. Young people get these drugs from older brothers and sisters.

14 They get them from friends. They also get them from Mom's and Dad's liquor cabinet or private stash.

The big question is: "Why do young people take drugs?" Let's look at the reasons that some young people gave.

People take drugs to forget their problems

But what if Linda gets drunk to forget her problems and is in a car accident? She could kill someone. What if her parents find out? What if she is sick? Linda has added to her list of problems.

People take drugs to be "cool"

Now think to yourself: What is so cool about damaging your brain? What is so cool about being so wasted that you can't remember where you've been or what you've done? Cool people don't cheat and steal so they can buy another hit of crack.

People take drugs to look older

It's tough to be young. Everyone treats you like a child. You want them to know how mature you are. You want everyone to know that you can handle whatever comes your way. But getting older is a natural process. People who are truly mature are able to say "No" to things that will mess up their life.

People take drugs to rebel against their parents

They think that they can hurt their parents by taking drugs. They want to see their parents in pain. Taking drugs usually does hurt their parents. It also hurts the people who take the drugs. Sometimes it can even kill them. Taking drugs to rebel hurts everybody.

People take drugs because their friends are doing it

Sometimes it's really hard to say "No" to a friend. But a true friend won't force you to do something you don't want to do. Are you the leader or the follower? You need to be a leader and tell your friends exactly where you stand. Every person is special. You don't have to do anything just because your friends do it. You can be the leader and suggest other fun things to do.

16 | ***People take drugs because they like the feeling it gives them***

Think about the things you like to do. Going to see a funny movie can give you a good feeling. Being around good friends can give you a good feeling. Many things in life can make you feel good. You can get high on life. It won't destroy you the way drugs can.

People take drugs to be popular

That means that you will be popular for taking drugs, not because people like you for yourself. What if you are arrested for taking drugs? The only places you'll be popular are in the newspaper, the court-room, or the juvenile center. You can be popular by being good at sports, by being nice to people, and many other ways. Taking drugs is not the only way to be popular.

People take drugs because they are curious

Answer this question: Would you stand on the railroad tracks and let the train hit you to see if it would hurt? Of course, you wouldn't! You know that the train could

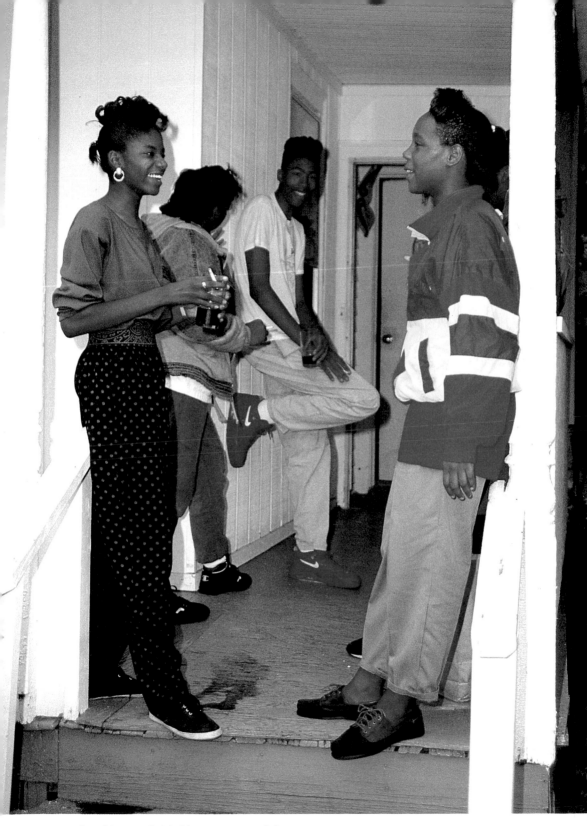

Smoking and drinking are part of the party scene.

18 hurt you or kill you. People also know that drugs can hurt them or kill them. It doesn't make sense to play with danger.

People think, "It can't happen to me"

Almost every day we hear about people who lose their job because of drug use. We hear about people who are kicked out of school for drugs. We also hear about people who die from a drug overdose. It happened to those people. It can happen to anyone who uses drugs. Ask addicts if they wanted to be addicts. Nobody takes drugs because they want to be addicted. Everyone who is an addict thought, "It can't happen to me." And now their life is a mess.

Young people take drugs for all of these reasons. They are curious. They want to be like the older kids.

Even the drugs alcohol and tobacco that are legal for adults are very dangerous for growing teenagers. From the time you are born, your body starts growing. Your body keeps growing until you are between the ages of nineteen and twenty-two. During this growing time, it is important to give your body only good things. Drugs

such as marijuana, alcohol, and tobacco
can really hurt a growing body.

The damage starts when a young person begins experimenting with drugs. Marijuana, alcohol, and tobacco are called "gateway drugs." They open the gate to harder drugs. Here is an example: A young body builds tolerance to alcohol. It takes more and more alcohol to get drunk. After a while, getting drunk takes too long. It becomes quicker and easier to smoke marijuana to get high. Then the body builds a tolerance to marijuana. The person looks for a quicker, stronger drug. The person moves on to cocaine or crack. Using tobacco, alcohol, or marijuana leads to using harder drugs. That's why they are called "gateway drugs."

A growing body can become addicted to a drug ten times faster than an adult body. So a little experiment with drugs often leads to regular use of a drug.

The body is still changing during the teen years. It builds a tolerance to a drug very fast. Then, as you know, it takes more of the drug to reach the same high. Next, the young body starts to need the drug.

After using drugs, the young body has a damaged heart. The body has a changed

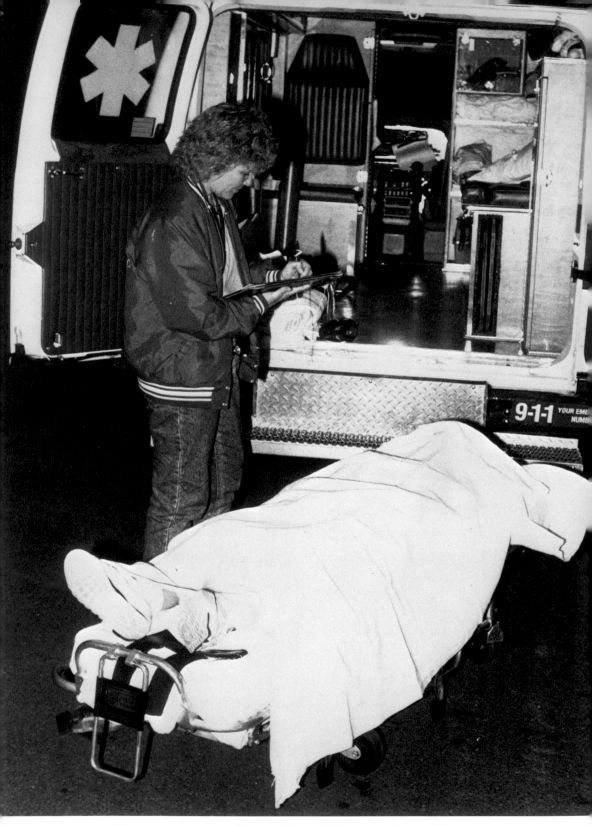

Teenagers may overdose on drugs without meaning to. Then
they become accident statistics.

brain. It has problems with its lungs, its eyes, and its muscles. The body may also have big problems with its *reproductive system*. That means that using drugs during the growing years may damage the ability to have children. This is another reason that taking drugs during the growing years is dangerous. By the time you stop growing, your body may be in bad shape. Then you have to spend the rest of your life with a damaged body.

Remember these things: Alcohol and tobacco are legal only for adults. Young bodies are still growing. They can become addicted to drugs much faster than adults. The damage to a growing body can be very serious.

Experimenting with tobacco, alcohol, and marijuana leads to the use of harder drugs such as cocaine and crack. People give many reasons for taking drugs. There are also many reasons not to take drugs. It's possible to get high on life!

A drug habit leads the addict to crime to get money for more crack or cocaine.

CHAPTER 3

Cocaine

We've learned that tobacco, marijuana, and alcohol are gateway drugs. They open the gate to harder drugs. Cocaine is one of those harderdrugs.

What is cocaine? Where does it come from? Why do people take cocaine? Here are some answers.

Cocaine is a very powerful stimulant. A stimulant makes your body work faster. It gives your body false energy. It speeds up your brain and your heart.

There are many names for cocaine. People call it "coke," "blow," or "snow." It is a white powder that people snort up the

23

24 nose to get high. Some people inject cocaine or smoke cocaine. Any way you take
it, it is a very dangerous drug.

Cocaine messes with your *central nervous system*. This system includes your
brain and spinal cord. The central nervous
system controls your entire body. When
cocaine mixes up your central nervous
system, your body doesn't know how to
operate properly.

Where does cocaine come from? It
comes from the *coca plant*. (Don't be con-
fused. The coca plant is different from the
cacao plant. The cacao plant gives us co-
coa and chocolate.) The leaves of the coca
plant contain a very small amount of cocaine.

The coca plant grows in the Andes
Mountains of South America. The coun-
tries of Peru and Bolivia grow a lot of
coca. The Inca Indians farm coca in the
mountains. They pick the coca leaves to
sell them.

It takes long hours and hard work to
pick the leaves. The Indians chew the coca
leaves to get the small amount of the drug
they contain. It helps them stay awake and
work more. Chewing the coca leaves is
also part of their religion. However, most
Incas live only to the age of thirty.

The Indians sell the coca leaves to drug dealers. The drug dealers turn the leaves into the white powder called cocaine. But how do they get cocaine from the coca leaves? Let's find out.

The cocaine is taken out of the coca leaves by mixing *kerosene* or *acid* with them. The mixing of coca leaves and acid is called *purifying*. So, when you take cocaine you are taking more than just cocaine powder.

Cocaine is taken from the coca leaves in two steps. First, the coca leaves are put in a press or steel drum with acid and crushed into a mash called "pasta." Then the pasta is mixed with another acid. The product is the white powder called cocaine. A person who snorts it is also snorting acid.

Hold on, our story is far from over. Other things besides acid are added to the cocaine that is sold on the street. Drug dealers add sugar, heroin, baby powder or other drugs to the powder. Here is an example: A drug dealer has one pound of cocaine. He mixes in a pound of sugar and heroin. Now he has two pounds of cocaine to sell. He will make much more money. The buyer never knows what he's getting. The buyer is even more at risk.

26 Cocaine is not a "new" drug in the United States. It was discovered more than 100 years ago. Scientists were searching for new medicines. They learned that the Incas chewed the leaves for energy. They also found that purifying the coca leaves gave them the strong drug called cocaine. Scientists thought that it was a harmless cure for some illnesses.

People began to realize that cocaine was not harmless. In 1906 a law was passed that limited the use of cocaine in medicines. However, cocaine can be used as a painkiller (anesthetic) in certain operations on the nose and throat. It makes the skin numb. Only special doctors are allowed to use cocaine for operations. It is used in very small amounts.

Cocaine is a very dangerous drug. We have known that for over 100 years. That is why it is against the law. Still, many people decide to use cocaine.

That is where the drug dealer comes in. Cocaine is a strong drug. People become dependent on it. The drug dealer knows this. A drug-dependent person will pay any price to get the high. A dealer may charge $60 to $100 for a single gram of cocaine. Often the dealer gives cocaine to kids free.

Cocaine is expensive: A few hits cost a lot of dollars.

If a kid takes it and becomes addicted, the dealer has a new customer. Then he can charge the kid high prices for the coke.

For many years cocaine was not a problem in the United States. In 1914 it became against the law. Then the drug went on a long vacation. The public stopped using it because it was not safe.

28   Why is it so popular now? It's popular for many reasons. During the 1960s and 1970s young people began using drugs a lot. It was the "cool" thing to do. Cocaine was a popular drug because of its power. Cocaine was also expensive. Most people couldn't afford it at first.

Then the 1980s came along. Cocaine was called the "champagne of drugs." That meant that it was the best drug. It meant that cocaine was a drug for rich, trendy people. Movie stars and rock stars were using cocaine. Professional basketball, football, and baseballl players were using cocaine. Rich businessmen and women were using cocaine. It was the drug for "glamorous" people.

The "glamorous" people of the 1980s thought that cocaine had no down side. They thought it only made life better. They had enough money to pay for the expensive drug. Using cocaine was a sign that you were rich and famous.

Cocaine does have a down side, though. John Belushi was a popular actor on "Saturday Night Live." In 1982, John Belushi died when he took cocaine mixed with heroin.

Len Bias was a star basketball player in college. He signed a contract with the

Boston Celtics. There was a party in his honor. At the party, he snorted cocaine. His heart couldn't take it. He died.

Cocaine can kill a person. Still, many people think that cocaine is glamorous. Not only rich people, but other people too.

Remember these things: Alcohol, tobacco, and marijuana are gateway drugs. They can lead to using cocaine. Cocaine is called "coke," "blow," and "snow." It is a very powerful stimulant that acts on your central nervous system.

Cocaine comes from the coca plant, which grows in the mountains of South America. Adding kerosene or acid to the coca leaves is called purifying. You get cocaine by purifying coca leaves.

Cocaine is very expensive. Actors, famous athletes, and rich business people made cocaine popular. They thought it had no bad side. But cocaine can kill even a healthy person.

When police identify a crack house the dealers and buyers are
hauled off to jail.

CHAPTER 4

What Is Crack?

Snorting cocaine up your nose is not the only way to take cocaine. A method called *freebasing* changes the cocaine powder so that you can smoke it.

In freebasing, powdered cocaine is mixed with ether (a liquid that is also used as a painkiller). The powder is mixed with other chemicals too. A cocaine base is formed. It is called freebase. It acts on your body faster than powdered cocaine because you smoke it. The drug goes to your lungs and then to your brain. It happens very fast.

Freebasing is very risky. It causes hallucinations. You see things that aren't really there. It causes paranoia. You think the world is out to get you.

32   Freebasing also causes health problems. It can cause a heart attack. It can make you have a stroke. Freebasing messes up your lungs, your brain, your heart, and your life.

Richard Pryor, the famous comedian, was freebasing in 1982. The ether he was using exploded. His body was badly burned. He almost died.

Freebasing is extremely dangerous. So someone came up with a "better idea." Crack was invented. It is much more powerful than cocaine or freebase. It makes you high faster. And it is easy to make.

Crack is made by mixing cocaine with baking soda and water. It is boiled into a paste. Then it hardens. The result is a "rock" of crack. It's called crack because of the sound it makes when you smoke it. It looks like a small white chip. It can be made in any kitchen. The process of making crack is much safer than freebasing. Many people who freebased in the past now use crack instead.

Crack is a ready-to-smoke product. The dealers can sell it for $10 or $20 apiece. A hit of crack is cheaper than a hit of powdered cocaine. The high is much more intense. And younger people can afford it.

What Is Special About Crack?

What is so special about crack? Why is it getting so much attention? There are many reasons. More and more people are becoming addicted to it. The crime rate has gone up. Thousands of crack babies are born each year. There are many more reasons. Let's look at these reasons more closely.

You know that crack is cheap. It is sold on the streets, ready to smoke. You can buy it almost everywhere. That is why crack is called the "fast food of drugs." In some cities, buying crack is as easy as getting a hamburger at McDonald's.

34   You also know that thousands of people are addicted to crack. They buy a lot of it. And addicts always want more. So the drug dealers need to buy more cocaine to make the crack. They buy it from drug smugglers in South America. The country of Peru grows 33 tons of coca leaves each year. The country of Bolivia grows 38 tons each year. The coca leaves are turned into cocaine. Much of this cocaine comes to the United States. Then the dealers turn the cocaine into crack. That's a lot of dangerous drugs floating around!

A single hit of crack costs less than a single hit of powder cocaine. A rock of crack costs $5, $10, or $20. Cocaine is sold in grams. A gram costs $60 to $100. The low price of crack makes it easy for everybody to buy.

What is the real cost, though? Crack smokers get high and then "crash." The users want more crack to get over the depression they feel. Then they have to spend another $10 or $20 to get more crack. If they buy crack ten times in a week, they have spent between $100 and $200. Powder cocaine seems to cost more than crack. But, in the end, crack costs more because the users need more of it.

Crack makes addicts faster than any other drug.

Crack began to get attention around 1985. Its low price makes it special. Almost anyone can afford a $10 piece. Crack is also special because the high is very intense. The drug is smoked in a pipe. It goes straight to the lungs and brain. People become addicted quickly. So crack became very popular. Within a few months crack was in most major cities. Now it is very easy to buy even in small cities and towns.

36   Crack is also special because the dealers are very well organized. They have set up special houses for their customers. The houses are called "crack houses." The dealers sell crack in these houses. The users also smoke crack in these houses. It gives them a place to go and get high. They don't have to take a chance of getting caught on the street. They also don't have to do it at home. The crack houses are very handy for users.

Cocaine powder is snorted up the nose. Some of it is absorbed by the body. It takes the drug three or four minutes to reach the brain. Crack is different here too. It is smoked, as you know. But crack reaches the lungs and brain in *less than 10 seconds*. Whereas cocaine takes a few minutes, crack takes only a few seconds.

Cocaine powder will keep you high for two or three *hours*. Crack will keep you high for only five or ten *minutes*. The crack high is followed by a big low. The user becomes very depressed. The user feels sad and alone. The depression is hard to endure. The user buys another rock of crack and smokes it to forget the depression. That is how people become addicted so quickly. As soon as they crash, they want to get high again.

Because it is smoked, crack is stronger than powder cocaine. The strength of crack makes it very addictive. Crack is ten times more addictive than cocaine that is snorted. Some users say that they were hooked by the first or second hit. *Crack is the most addictive drug known to man.* That is another reason it is special compared to other drugs. That is also why it's so scary.

People can overdose on crack too. An overdose can happen at any time. It can happen a few minutes after using. It can happen an hour after using. An overdose happens when the body gets too much cocaine. You lose control of your body. You begin to have body spasms called *seizures*. You can pass out or go into a coma. If you don't get medical help, you will die.

Crack hurts everybody. It is dangerous for many reasons. Since it hit the streets, crime has gone way up. Crack houses are guarded by teenagers with guns. Street gangs get involved too.

Crack users run out of money. They steal to get money to buy more. Teenagers have started selling drugs to make money. Some also sell their bodies for sex to get money to buy more crack.

38   People on crack feel as if they can take on the world. They feel very powerful. They get angry over little things. Often they become violent. That is why crack is blamed for a big increase in the number of murders. The borough of Queens in New York City has had a 25 percent increase in murders. In Washington, DC, the murder rate has doubled.

A crack house is sealed up after a raid so that it cannot go back into business.

Crack dealers can make millions of   *39*
dollars. The dealers fight over territory to
sell crack. They want more territory to get
to more customers. Street gangs in Los
Angeles are having a war over crack. In
1987 the gangs killed 387 people.

Drug dealers and users are also having
a war with the police. The police want the
crime to end. But 60 percent of all crimes
can be related to drug use. If people
stopped taking drugs, the crime rate would
drop.

The crack problem in Miami, Florida, is
big. Half of all drug arrests in Miami are
related to crack.

The police blame crack for the increase
in teen crime also. Since crack became
popular, crime has gone way up. People
turn to robbery, drug dealing, or prostitu-
tion to earn money for crack. The dealers
are making millions of dollars. They murder others who get in their way.

Crack is also special because of the lives
it destroys. Pregnant women who use
crack harm their baby. The baby is born
addicted to the drug. These babies are
called "crack babies." In 1989 New York
City had 3,837 crack babies. Chicago had
1,095 crack babies. Los Angeles had 2,284
crack babies. More than 200,000 crack

When a parent is hooked on drugs, the children face a sad future.

babies are born each year in the United States.

Crack babies have problems with their lungs. They have problems with their heart. They need more medical attention than regular babies. Many crack babies have mental problems too. They have trouble adjusting to everyday life because of crack.

This drug doesn't care who you are. Young people and old people use crack. Rich people and poor people use crack. Black people and white people use crack. Even mothers and fathers use crack.

Child abuse and neglect have risen because of crack. Parents who use it can't think about their children. They forget to feed the kids. They spend the money on drugs instead of food. They get angry at the kids very easily too. The number of child abuse cases has risen 36 percent since crack came around. That doesn't mean that the parents don't love the kids. It means that crack is messing up their mind. They love the high that crack gives them. Crack addicts have no control over themselves. They need professional help.

Remember these things: crack is smoked. It is sold for a low price. Anybody can afford to buy it. All types of people smoke crack. It is ten times more powerful than powder cocaine. Even healthy people can overdose on crack.

Crime rates have risen because of crack. It makes people feel powerful and violent. People steal, cheat, lie, or sell their bodies for crack. It is the *most addictive* drug known to man. Pregnant women and parents who use crack are destroying the lives of many children. That is what makes crack so special. That's why crack gets so much attention.

In filthy surroundings, crack addicts gather to smoke the drug in secret.

Why People Use Crack

*D*rugs have been popular for almost thirty years. They play a part in everyday life. Television shows such as "Miami Vice" show the exciting, fast-paced life of cocaine. Movies show young people getting drunk or going to parties and getting high. They make it look like fun. And for years music has been saying that drugs are cool.

Eric Clapton had a hit record called "Cocaine" with these words: "When the day is done and you want to run—Cocaine." Groups like the Rolling Stones and the Beatles also had songs about the good effects of drugs. In the 1980s Pink Floyd had "The Wall." The song "Comfortably Numb" became popular. Twisted Sister sang: "We gotta fight for our right to party!" And Motley Crue now sings about "Dr. Feelgood." Too many people accept drug use as a part of life. They think that

44 taking drugs is "no big deal." Some music, movies, and TV shows seem to support that attitude. But all of those people are wrong!

People use crack for different reasons. They think that getting high will make their problems go away. But over 80 percent of the people who try crack become addicted to it. Crack damages a person's lungs and brain. It makes the heart work harder and faster. It causes people to see things that aren't there. It also makes people violent. Crack doesn't make problems go away. It causes more problems.

People take crack because they think it's glamorous. They take it because it's cheap. They take it because it makes them feel powerful.

Crack is not glamorous. People sit around in dirty, smelly crack houses to get high. They sell their bodies for sex so they can buy crack. Users steal from their family. There's nothing glamorous about crack.

Crack is not as cheap as people think. A crack high lasts only five or ten minutes. The user wants to get high again right away. Crack ends up costing more than other drugs. The user needs more of it, more often.

Crack is easy to make. It is easy to buy. **45**
People get crack from their friends or
people they work with. They take it to be a
part of the "in" crowd.

There's a big problem with this excuse
for using crack. When you are arrested by
the police, where will your friends be?
When you are fired from your job, where
will your coworkers be? The "in" crowd
disappears when the going gets rough.

Some people say that crack makes your
sex life better. They may be right, at first.
But repeated use of crack often causes
impotence in men. That means that their
penis can't get erect. Then they can't have
sex at all.

Some people trade sex for crack. And
the number of sexual diseases has gone
up. Health workers say that sexual diseases are spreading because people are
using drugs such as crack.

Every person has three basic drives.
These drives are for food, water, and sex. A
crack addict always needs crack. The need
for the drug overpowers the basic drives
for food, water, and sex. That just proves
that crack will not make your sex life better. It will make you forget about food,
water, and sex.

When a teenager begins to neglect the important things—even eating—he may have a drug problem.

CHAPTER 7

Crack and You

*P*eople on crack change their whole lives. We know that using crack leads to crime. People steal from their family and friends. Crack users lie and cheat to get money to buy it. Other things also happen.

Drug users start hanging out with other drug users. They leave their old friends behind. Crack users lose interest in school. They don't care about work except to get money. They don't care about how they look. Drug users start dressing sloppy and not washing. They don't care about being around other people.

Crack smokers destroy their body. Your brain is the control center for your entire

48 body. When crack affects your brain it changes the way your eyes work. Bright light starts to hurt your eyes. Objects look fuzzy. Some crack smokers see floating objects from the corners of their eyes. Some users see little rings of light around objects. These are called "snow" lights. The crack smoker may also see two of everything.

The lungs and throat are also in trouble. Crack smoking can cause sore throat. It can also lead to an illness called bronchitis. This makes it hard to breathe.

Smoking crack makes your body weak. Many users don't get hungry. They would rather get high than eat. So they don't eat food. Then they lose weight. The body becomes weak without food. The body can't fight off diseases when it is weak. That is how crack smokers get sick.

Crack users start having hallucinations. They see things that aren't there. They become paranoid. They think that everyone is out to get them. Crack also messes up your heart. It makes the heart work faster. Blood pressure goes up. Your body temperature also goes up. The body becomes weak because of the drugs. So does the heart. Using crack can make you have

a heart attack. Even young, healthy people
have heart attacks when they use crack.

Remember that crack users also get
depressed without the drug. They get
moody. One minute they are happy. The
next minute they are mean. Crack users
begin to spend more time alone. Crack
becomes the most important thing. They
forget about hobbies. They don't care
about school or work. Crack addicts also
forget about their family and friends. They
don't care about anything but getting high
on crack.

Getting high makes them depressed.
The depresssed, lonely feeling is bad.
Some crack users try to commit suicide to
escape the crash that comes after every
high. People kill themselves because of
this drug.

Good friends and playing sports are a big help in avoiding the dangers of drugs.

CHAPTER 8

What Can You Do?

What can you do about crack? First of all, you can stay far away from it. You can say "No"!

Why should you say "No"? Because you have read this book. You know what smoking crack can do.

How can you say "No"? There are many ways to let people know that you don't do drugs. You can say "No" a hundred different ways. You can hang out with people who don't do drugs. You can avoid places where you know drugs will be. Most of all, you have to be strong. Let people know how you feel about drugs. If they say: "You're afraid!" you can say: "Yes, I am afraid. Messing with crack is stupid. Messing with any drug is stupid!"

52 How can you help someone on crack? Well, you are reading this book. You are educating yourself. That is a great first step. You know the signs to look for in a crack smoker:

- changes friends
- doesn't care about work or school
- loses weight
- can't sleep
- can't concentrate
- gets angry easily
- runs out of money quickly

If you want to, you can share what you know about crack. Your friend may not have correct information. Be sure you talk when your friend is not high. There's something else you need to know. Sharing information will help. But this person needs professional help.

You can also be a good listener. Let your friend express feelings and tell you about problems.

If you want to help your friend, don't lend money. Don't go to places where there will be drugs. Invite your friend to drug-free places.

You can also talk to your friend's parents. Let them know what you think. Don't worry about "narcing" on your friends. In the long run you will be helping.

A person addicted to crack needs professional help. There are many places you can turn to. You can call most hotline numbers twenty-four hours a day. They can help you or tell you where to find help in your area of the country.

- The Cocaine Hotline: 1-800-COCAINE (262-2463)
- The National Institute on Drug Abuse Hotline: 1-800-662-HELP
- Narcotics Anonymous: 818-780-3951 (look in your local phone book)
- National Secret Witness: 1-800-73-CRIME

There is also help and support for the family members of drug addicts. If someone in your family is an addict, you are not alone. There are places you can call too.

- COCANON Family Groups: 213-859-2206 (look in your local phone book)
  P.O. Box 64742-66
  Los Angeles, CA 90064

- Families Anonymous: 818-989-7841 (look in your local phone book)
  P.O. Box 528
  Van Nuys, CA 91408

54   • Nar-Anon: 213-547-5800
World Office
P.O. Box 2562
Palos Verdes Peninsula, CA 92704

For more information on drugs:

• National Clearinghouse for Alcohol and
Drug Information
P.O. Box 2345
Rockville, MD 20852
301-468-2600

• American Council for Drug Education
204 Monroe Street
Rockville, MD 20852
301-294-0600

• National Federation of Parents for Drug-
Free Youth
8730 Georgia Avenue
Silver Spring, MD 20910
1-8000-554-KIDS (5437)

• NIDA Clearinghouse for Drug Information
P.O. Box 416
Kensington, MD 20795

Fact Sheet

- 90 percent of crack users also used alcohol, tobacco, and marijuana.
- 93 percent of all people who have tried cocaine used marijuana first.
- 100 percent of marijuana nonusers had *not* used cocaine in the last month.
- 13,938 cocaine-related emergencies (over-doses) reported in 1986.
- Cocaine-related deaths rose 126 percent (1983-1986).
- 25 million Americans have tried cocaine.

56

- *Crack is the most addicting substance known to man.*
- Bolivia grows 38 tons of coca leaves per year.
- Peru grows 33 tons of coca leaves per year.
- The U.S. consumes 60 percent of the cocaine produced.
- Crack increases pulse rate 30 to 50 percent.
- Crack increases blood pressure 15 to 20 percent.
- 38 percent of cocaine mothers have miscarriages.
- Cocaine mothers have greater numbers of premature babies.
- Crack babies have 3 times the chance of incurring SIDS (Sudden Infant Death Syndrome).
- Since crack, murders in Queens have risen 25 percent.
- Murders in Washington, DC, have doubled since crack appeared.
- Crack murders by street gangs in Los Angeles numbered 387 in 1987.
- Crack is 10 times more powerful than cocaine.
- $39 billion was spent on cocaine in 1985.

- Cocaine abusers are at high risk for mental illness.
- 82 percent of crack users reported an immediate compulsion to use it again right away.
- 5,000 people "try" some form of cocaine each day.
- 5,000,000 people use some form of cocaine regularly.
- 200,000 crack babies are born each year in the United States.
- Since 1985 the amount of smuggled cocaine has risen 500 percent.
- 60 percent of all crime is drug-related.
- Today's marijuana is 10 to 12 times more potent than the marijuana of the 1960s.
- A gram of cocaine is enough for 30 to 50 lines.
- A gram of cocaine is enough to keep two people high for many hours.
- An ounce of cocaine sells for $1,800 to $2,500 on the street. This is more than six times the price of gold.
- 90 percent of callers on 800-Cocaine report bad physical, social, and mental effects.
- In 1988 there were 15,000 medical emergencies involving crack.

58

- Drug use is higher among those who have not finished high school.
- Cocaine and marijuana use among students who cut class four or more times is almost twice as high as among those who have not cut class.
- In 1985 there were 5.8 million regular users of cocaine. In 1989 there were 2.9 million regular users.
- The amount of cocaine used is going up every year because those who use cocaine are using much more of it.

Glossary
Explaining New Words

chemical dependency an illness that happens when someone needs a drug. Without the drug, the person suffers withdrawal.

cocaine a stimulant made from the leaves of the coca plant.

crack the most addictive drug known to man. Made from cocaine. It is smoked. It is deadly. It is illegal.

depression a state of feeling sad and alone.

ether liquid used to freebase cocaine.

experimenting trying drugs to see how they feel. Often leads to regular use of drugs.

60 **freebasing** a dangerous process of mixing cocaine so it can be smoked.

gateway drugs alcohol, tobacco, and marijuana. Lead to the use of harder drugs like cocaine and crack.

hallucination hearing, seeing, or feeling things that are not real. Can be brought on by drugs like crack.

overdose Harmful effects of taking too much of a drug. A deadly or toxic amount of drugs.

paranoia an unreal feeling of distrust. Thinking that everyone is out to get you. Can be brought on by crack.

purifying mixing coca leaves with acid to make cocaine powder.

reproductive system the sex organs of the male and female body that allow people to create children.

stimulant drug that speeds up the work of the body. Cocaine and crack are stimulants.

tolerance when the body becomes accustomed to a drug. With tolerance a body needs more and more of a drug to get the same high.

withdrawal changes in the body such as chills, fever, trembling, cramps, or convulsions when dependent or addicted.

For Further Reading

Easy To Read

Berger, Gilda. *Crack, the New Drug Epidemic.* New York: Franklin Watts, 1987.

Twist, Clint. *The Crack and Cocaine Epidemic.* New York: Franklin Watts, 1989.

Woods, Geraldine. *Cocaine.* New York: Franklin Watts, 1985.

Hyppo, Marion, and Hastins, Jill. *An Elephant in the Living Room.* Minneapolis: Compcare Publications.

Seixas, Judith. *Alcohol—What It Is, What It Does.* New York: Glenwillow Books, 1977.

62 Scott, Sharon. *How to Say No and Keep
       Your Friends.* Amherst, MA: Human
       Resource Development Press, Inc.,
       1988.
Scott, Sharon. *When to Say Yes and Make
       More Friends.* Amherst, MA: Human
       Resource Development Press, Inc.,
       1988.

Not as Easy to Read, But Worth the Effort

Gold, Mark, M.D. *The Facts about Drugs
       and Alcohol.* New York: Bantam
       Books, 1988.
Gold, Mark, M.D. *800-Cocaine.* New York:
       Bantam Books, 1984. (Look for *800-
       Cocaine* with a special chapter on
       crack.)

Index

64

About the Author

Rodney Peck is a graduate of Central Michigan University. He has worked in drug prevention and education with the America's PRIDE program for five years. He has presented workshops on peer pressure, drug education, self-esteem, and effective communication. His work with PRIDE has taken him to Canada, the U.S. Virgin Islands, throughout the United States, and to Belize. Currently he is a Peace Corps Volunteer in Belize, assigned to the drug education program known as PRIDE/Belize.

Photo Credits

Cover Photo: Gamma-Liaison © Frank Fischer
Photos on pages 2, 6, 12, 17, 20, 22, 27, 40, 46: Stuart Rabinowitz; pages 30, 35, 38, 42, Wide World; page 50, Stephanie FitzGerald

Design & Production; Blackbirch Graphics, Inc.